I0157739

Are You

Bold
enough to
BELIEVE?

Willie Howell

Are Your Bold Enough To Believe

Are You

Bold

enough to

BELIEVE?

Unless otherwise indicated all scriptural quotations are taken from the King James Version of the Bible

Are You Bold Enough To Believe
Copyright ©2012
Willie Howell

Printed in the United States of America
Library of Congress – Catalogued in Publication Data

ISBN 978-0-9839248-8-3
Published by Jabez Books
(A Division of Clark's Consultant Group)
www.clarksconsultantgroup.com

<u>Acknowledgements</u>

In writing this book, I was inspired by the Spirit of God and encouraged by my wife of 30 years, Brigette, who has stood by me with her loving care, and Dr. Roxanne Tyroch, a wonderful friend for many years. And to my dear friends and confidants who would not let me fail to do what God has placed in my heart to do, Danny and Olivia Garcia of Industrial Power Solutions. They have been my strong help and support throughout the years.

To each of them who supported and encouraged me to write this book, I owe my deepest gratitude to. I may not have undertaken such a great task without your help.

My mentor and former spiritual father, Pastor Charles Nieman, pastor of the Abundant Living Faith Center in El Paso Texas, who has a membership of over 15,000, has been my example of dedication and excellence for years -- his relentless attention to detail, untiring research for accurate teaching of the gospel, and the love and devotion he has for the people of God is a tremendous example of a man with great character and integrity.

It is my prayer in writing this book that all who read it may walk away from reading this book with a better understanding for the words that they allow to proceed out of their mouths.

Special thanks to Devin Johnson who has been a close friend and prayer partner for years and to my pastor and great man of God in his own right, Pastor Lemuel Brown of Kingdom Light World Ministry.

Elder Willie Howell
Ordained Elder of Kingdom Light World Ministry

Table of Contents

Section 1

Harness Your Real Power

Changing the way you speak is the key.

Changing the way you speak for a better life is paramount to your future and your quality of life, therefore, it is extremely important for you to harness the power that is in your mouth.

Paul tells us in II Corinthians 4:13 that we have the same spirit of faith that Jesus has and in I Corinthians 12:9a that the spirit of God gives us the spirit of faith, and again in Romans 12:3b that God has given to every man that believes, the measure of faith. This is all the faith we are going to get. So what you must do now is develop what you have, and the way you do that is through your use of faith.

This is the same faith that Jesus used to surrender His will to die on the cross for you. It is the same faith that Jesus used to go into the pit of hell to defeat Satan and on the third day, rise again. It is the same faith that He developed and given to you for you to use -- "Looking unto Jesus the **author** and **finisher** of our faith" (Hebrews 12:2).

What is an author? One who originates or creates.

What is a finisher? One who completes and perfects. Jesus is the originator, the creator, "All things were made by him; and without him was not anything made that was made; and Jesus is the finisher" (John 1:3). "I have glorified thee on the earth: I have finished the work which thou gave me to do" (John 17:4).

Paul goes on to say that it is according to the written scripture, Psalms 116:10a, I believe, therefore have I spoken. Paul quotes this verse and then he says: We also believe, and therefore speak.

According to Hebrews 11:6, it is **impossible** to please God without **faith**, because he that comes to God must believe that God **is**. The question that comes to mind is what is God any way? John said in John 4:24, that God is a **spirit**: and they that worship Him must worship Him in spirit and in truth.

Section 2

The Worship of God

Your heartfelt thanks and expression of joy to God is worship of God.

How do you worship God in spirit? First of all, you are a spirit, you have a soul, and you live in a body (I Thessalonians 5:23). And the words that you speak, Jesus said are spirit. In John 6:63, Jesus explains the power of the spirit. He says this; it is the spirit that makes life, and the flesh profit little: the words that I speak unto you, they are spirit, and it is they that bring life.

You are a spirit and the words that you speak come from your spirit, so you worship God In spirit and in truth. You worship God with your **words**, and they must be spoken in truth by faith.

Remember this, because your words are spirit and because you are in a fleshly body that is subject to sin; your words can take on two positions.

The first being words of life, as already stated and the second being words of death and bondage according to Proverbs 18:21, death and life are in the power of the tongue, and in Proverbs 6:2, you are snared, held captive, by the words that you speak.

You have this ability because of the nature of being that you are. You are a three part being created in the image and the likeness of God and given the ability to speak words, which come from your spirit, which has the power to bring life or death. Man is the only being that has this ability.

Section 3

Who is God?

H e is all that the mind can conceive and greatly above it.

God is the God of all flesh, and there is nothing that He can't do (Jeremiah 32:27). In Genesis 17:1b, God declares that He is the Almighty God or you could say it this way -- He is the God of all powerful strength. And in Exodus 3:14, God tells Moses, I AM THAT I AM. Another way said, I am that which causes things to be. Everything was created by God and without Him, nothing can exist.

In Colossians, chapter 1, starting at verse 16, you find out that all things were made by God, everything, everything that is in heaven and everything that is in the earth; visible and invisible, that is not manmade.

All spirits were made by God: thrones, dominions, principalities, and powers, all were made by God and without Him nothing could exist, including Satan.

Section 4

What Are You?

You come from the DNA of God, created by His Son, and guided by His Spirit.

You were created in the image and likeness of God, and given power over all the earth (Genesis 1:26 and Ephesians 5:1). You are commanded to be followers or imitators of God, as dear children.

That means that you are called to act like God, speak like God, and live like a child of God.

If you were the son of Queen Elizabeth and you were next in line for the throne, wouldn't you be expected to act like, speak like, look like, and live like a person of power?

As a child of God, you represent power and authority. That means you have the right to declare a thing and the right to enforce it. As well, you represent two levels of leadership: the office of a king and the office of a priest.

Revelation 1:6 says that we have been made kings and priests unto God, the Son and His Father, who is God, the Father. And again in Revelation 5:10, we are made kings and priests unto God. In addition, I Peter 2:9 says, we are a chosen generation and a royal priesthood.

In Revelation 19:16, it says that Jesus is King of kings and Lord of lords. And in Hebrews 7:17, He is called a priest for ever after the order of Melchizedek. This means that you have the power to declare a law, enforce it and minister forgiveness, "all under one hat."

Now, your words are very important because of your position as a leader. They are so important that Jesus made this statement in Matthew 12:36, "I say unto you, that every idle word that men shall speak, they shall give account thereof in the Day of Judgment."

Verse 37, "For by your words you shall be justified, and by your words you shall be condemned."

Notice here that you have the ability to speak words that have no assignment as well as words that can be constructed. These "no assignment" words are words that are inactive, unemployed, and not given anything to do.

These are words that take up space in the air once they have been spoken. They take up the time it takes to create them, and they take up energy from your spirit.

Section 5

Your Words Create Your Life

You and your words are one, just as God and His words are one.

If we are called to be good stewards of money, we should be no less good stewards of our words, because our words are more important than our money, due to the fact that our words create our livelihood.

In Proverbs 6:2, it says this, "You are snared (bound up and held captive) with the words of your mouth; you are taken (snatched up) with the words of your mouth.

Proverbs 18:21, "Death and life are in the power of the tongue: and they that love it shall eat the fruit thereof." You have the ability to bring life or death just by speaking a thing with your mouth. Jesus said in John 6:63, "It is the spirit that gives life, not the flesh: the words that I speak unto you, they are spirit and they are life."

Since we are created in the image and likeness of God, we have the same ability as Christ, but with one addition, we can also speak death because of the sin of Adam.

This is another reason for us to watch what we say, because we now have the ability to build up or tear down, to create and to destroy, all by the power that is in our mouths.

The old saying, "Sticks and stones may break my bones, but words will never hurt me," is not a statement of truth. Words can hurt you and much more.

Section 6

Getting the Correct Words in Your Mouth

Words do not have to be many to be effective.

In Matthew 12:34, Jesus said whatever is in your heart in abundance is going to come out of your mouth. Well, if this is correct, how do you get words of faith and power in your heart?

In II Timothy 2:15, we are told to **study**, in Joshua 1:8, we are told to **meditate**, in John 5:39, we are told to **search** -- search what, search the scriptures. After doing that you must believe the Word of God. Jesus said this, "If you can believe, all things will be possible to him that will believe" (Mark 9:23).

Many lives have been changed because people have chosen to believe in what could and can be just by removing the prefix "UN" from the word belief. Romans 10:10 says it is with the heart that a man believes. Mark 11:23 says this, "If you believe that the things you say shall come to pass (be obeyed, carried out, and preformed), you shall have whatsoever you say." In Mark 11:24, Jesus says this, "When you speak, believe that it will be done and it will."

Why should you do these things? David said in Psalms 119:130, that the entrance of the Word of God gives enlightenment and understanding to you. And in Psalms 119:11, David says it this way. "Thy word have I hid in my heart, that I might not sin against thee."

When you study, meditate, believe, and search the Word of God, God is able to get behind your words and confirm them; because it is God who makes your words productive unto doing what you say. In I Kings 1:14b, God says this, "I also will come in after you, and confirm your words." In Isaiah 44:26 (keeping with the context of God speaking), He says this. It is he who confirms the word of his servant, and performs the counsel of his messengers.

In Mark 16:20, we see that it is the Lord that went with His disciples to confirm their words with signs following. And according to I Samuel 3:19, all God need from you is faith in Him and He will not let your words fall to the ground, or become idle or inactive.

If there is one thing that the Bible encourages, it is belief. Why? Because if you can remove the prefix "UN" from belief, you will stop three things from having power over you. This is what I mean if you allow UN to remain in effect, you become opposed to what God says about you. You become the opposite of every good thing that God says you are, and you negate His power in your life and you remove His presence from you as well.

Your faith walk with God depends on your ability to allow God to walk with you and get behind your words and use His supernatural ability to affect your natural.

Don't become one who removes, negates, and opposes the love of God for you.

Section 7

Connecting Your Word with God's Word

God wants to use your words in the same manner that He uses His words.

He wants them to be truthful, faith-filled, and from the heart. When they are, He gets behind them and makes them His words, and when they become His words, they become productive as according to Isaiah 46:10. They will declare the end from the beginning, and in Isaiah 55:11, as the word goes out of your mouth, it will not return void, but they will accomplish that which you have spoken, so in effect, you are able to call things into your life which did not

31

exist, before you spoke them, Romans 4:17.

Now, when you get the Word of God in your heart, you give your mouth the ability to speak what is in there, be it the Word of God, the word of man or the word of Satan, and whatever is in there is the thing that will come out of your mouth. In Matthew 12:34B, Jesus says this, "Out of the abundance of the heart, the mouth will speak. Your words give you the ability to be a worshiper of God (John 4:24) or an enemy of God (John 3:18B).

Section 8

The Content of the Heart

Whatever you allow yourself to believe and become happy with, will pinpoint where you are spiritually.

Not only does your heart give your mouth the ability to speak, it also reveals the thing that you are thinking -- for as he thinks in his heart, so is he (Proverbs 23:7A).

Jesus said in Matthew 15:11 that it is not that which goes into the mouth that defiles a man, but that which comes out of the mouth, this is the thing that defiles him. Whatever you allow to become your most dominant thought in your mind, is the thing that will rule what you say. That which you speak, will become the thing that will govern your life.

The moment you say, I can't or I do not believe this or that, you place yourself in opposition to what you could be, and you remove all of the possible things that you could do, as well as negate all of the ability that God gave you to do them.

Proverbs 4:23 says, "Guard your heart with all diligence; for out of it are the issues of life." If you allow someone who does not know you to dictate what your life should be like, you give that person the power to remove, negate, and be opposed to what you should be. And if you allow that, you, in fact, become opposed to what you can do, and negate your own ability, and become in opposition to yourself also.

In other words, the thing that you have allowed to become your most dominant thought is the thing that will set the boundaries that you will live by. I have heard a pastor by the name of Pastor Charles Nieman say this many times, and it has become a very important part of my life; and it should be for yours also.

Section 9

Guarding Your Heart

Don't give the key to your mind to just anyone or anything, it is far too valuable for you to allow it to become a dumping ground for trash.

You must guard what you allow to go into your mind because you will begin to meditate on these things. And as you do, your mind will become full of these thoughts, so when you open your mouth to speak, whatever you have allowed to become dominate is the thing that will flow out of your mouth.

What do we see here? We see that your words are formed by the things you allow your mind to meditate on, and the more you think on these things, whether they are bad or good, the more your heart becomes full to overflowing. Therefore, when you speak, all of that stuff will flow out, and they will dictate how you will live your life and proclaim what you believe.

I submit to you, that the things you have said in previous days, is the reason your life is the way it is now. What you say today will dictate how you will live your life on tomorrow.

So if you want to change your tomorrow, you will have to change what you are saying today. Your heart is like a computer, garbage in, garbage out, righteousness in, righteousness out.

God is keeping a record of the words that are coming out of your mouth, "Every idle word that men shall speak, they shall give account thereof in the Day of Judgment (Matthew 12:36B). And He follows it up with verse 37, by saying, "For by your words you shall be justified, and by your words you shall be condemned."

In the book of James, chapter five, He warns us of the danger and the ability of man to speak both death and life out of our mouths. In fact, He likens the tongue to a small fire, when He says:

"The tongue is a small member but it speaks of great things, it can defile the whole body, and can set on fire the course of your natural life, and it gets that ability from the evil that comes from it."

This is the same tongue that we use to bless God and then turn around and curse man, which is made in the image and likeness of God. He is saying that your tongue is a small fire that can start a forest fire, and this should not be so because if you are a fig tree, how can you bear olive berries or if you are a fountain of sweet water, how can you bring up bitter water?

Even though you have the ability to speak both death and life, He says that you should desire to speak life and life only.

You are a follower of Christ, and you should speak as He speaks and believe as He believes (II Corinthians 4:13), that is what makes you a Christian (Acts 11:26).

You are a follower of the Lord, people should see Him in you, and the works that Jesus did. Case in point:

In the book of John, chapter 14:12, Jesus says this, He or she that believes in me, the works that I do shall he or she do also. Why is this? Because Jesus continued to say in part "C" of that verse, "...that He is going to the Father, and whatsoever you shall ask in His name, that is the thing that He will give unto you." Why? So that the Father may be glorified in the Son.

Section 10

Why In the Name of Jesus?

This is the name that has all power and it is the name that many fight against. It is a traffic guide to life, a sign post that you can chose to believe or reject.

The key here is that everything that you declare must be declared in the name of Jesus, because God has highly exalted Jesus, and made His name to be above every name that is named, so that in the name of Jesus, all other names shall bow, (acknowledging His Lordship over all things, because all things where made by Him -- "All things were made by him; and without him was not anything made that was made

(John 1:3). As we continue in Philippians 2:9-10...of things in heaven, and things in the earth, and things under the earth; there is no name that is named, anywhere, that is above the name of Jesus, all power and ability is in that name (Matthew 28:18).

Since everything was made by Him, everything is subject to Him and everything is known by Him and has no power over Him because He is the power, the knowledge, the understanding, and the ability that created everything -- nothing can exist, without Him. **When you use that name, you command the attention of everything that was made by the hand of Jesus.** All ears are open onto what you are about to say, this is when you must be on point because all things know when God speaks.

You have been given the ability to speak for God in the earth, through the name of Jesus because all things know Him, but not all things know who you are apart from Him.

Are Your Bold Enough To Believe

46

Section 11

Being a Believer

This is one of the main reasons you must be born again, so you can take your rightful place in the earth as one of the sons and daughters of Almighty God. So that when you speak, it is the same as God speaking, because you have fellowship (common interest and common desire).

This fellowship with the Father through the Son causes you to be led by the spirit because you have made Jesus the Lord of your life. Please remember that you have the DNA of God in you. You are not an accident or a plan gone wrong. And now that you are here, take possession of who you are. If you think you have it bad, look at where Jesus started out. He was born in a manger within a barn, wrapped in rags, surrounded by animals, and on a cold winter night, with no doctor or nurse to care for him.

God said that there is nothing that He cannot do; Jesus said that there is nothing that you cannot do, if you believe, and you can do it through Him. Philippians 4:13, says this, "I can do all things through Christ which strengthened me."

Remember, Jesus said this, "Whatever you ask the Father in my name, that I will do." It is not your ability that is at stake here, it is the ability of God. God is the power that will confirm the words that you speak not you. Your words need the power of God to bring them to pass; all He asks of you is for you to walk by faith and speak by faith.

Your dependency is not on you, but it is on God to do what He said He would do if you believe.

Section 12

Faith

Faith is the ability to open the door of opportunity that can only be seen by the eye of the spirit.

So what is faith? Let's look at Hebrews, chapter 11:1. It says, "Now faith is the substance of things hoped for, the evidence of things not seen." In the Amplified Bible, it says, "Now faith is the assurance (the confirmation, the title deed) of the things [we] hope for, being the proof of things [we] do not see and the conviction of their reality [faith perceiving as real fact what is not revealed to the senses]." I could put it this way:

Faith is the ability to command the spirit world to help me create the things that I desire, because James said in chapter 2:17, that Faith without good works is dead. Faith has to have actions of obedience on your part to back it up. Your obedience to the Word of God, combined with your belief is the thing that gives faith the ability to help you create the things you desire.

Jesus said in John, chapter 14:15, If you love me, keep (obey) my commandments. In Mark, chapter 9:23, Jesus says this, "If you can believe, all things are possible to him who believes."

Here is what is taking place when you call on faith: Jesus said in John, chapter 7, that if you abide in Him and His words abide in you, you can ask what you will, and it shall be done unto you.

You get the Word of God in your spirit and you believe it. Then you speak it out of your mouth into the spirit, with corresponding action and God's confirmation of His word in you, gives faith the ability to command the angels to go forth and help you create the thing that you desire. Remember this; there is no magic in the kingdom of God: there is only creative power through, wisdom, knowledge, and understanding.

Your belief and trust in the Word of God, combined with your corresponding actions gives the spirit of faith the ability to work with you. When He does, He brings with Him the power of heaven with Him to help you create the thing that you desire.

Case in point: In Luke, chapter 6:38, Jesus says, "Give and it shall be given unto you."

You activate the spirit of faith by your obedience to the Word. Then faith goes out to find a return source for your action. Now, if you just said, it shall be given unto me, and you did not do your part (which is to give), faith then has no back up, because you did not obey the Word of God, and God can't go behind you to confirm His Word in you. Therefore, faith can't release the angels to go and find a source of return for you.

Section 13

Faith, the Manager

The power, the force, and the momentum that is able to bring from the spirit world the ability to create what you desire in the natural.

Look at faith as a manager that manages the blessings of God and the blessings of God include: the angels, the Word, the blood, the name, and all of the spiritual forces of good.

When God confirms His Word in you, faith then can tell who He needs to go and help you to create the thing that you are asking for. These spiritual forces have been designed to act on words of faith. Satan's kingdom reacts on your words of fear and unbelief. Faith-filled words command the spirit of faith, and fear-filled words commands the spirit of fear.

The Bible says that angels, rather God's angels or fallen angels, they both listen for the words that give them power to act in your life (Psalm 103:20), which says, "Bless the Lord, ye his angels, that excel in strength, that do his commandments, hearkening unto the voice of his word."

In Daniel, chapter 10:12, the last part of the verse, the angel tells Daniel this:

"Your words were heard, and I am come for your words." In Luke, chapter 8, verse 12, we see that the kingdom of Satan comes to steal the Word of God, so that you do not have the ability to speak words of faith, and when you do not have the ability to speak words of faith, that leaves you speaking words of fear and unbelief, which gives the world of Satan the power they need to operate in your life.

Both kingdoms are waiting to hear what you will say, so that either will be in agreement with what you are saying, which will give them the authority to act. Just as faith is the manager of the blessings of God, fear is the manager of the curses and the spiritual forces that come to put you in bondage.

Section 14

Where It All Starts

Can anything start without a source and can there be a source without a desire.

You see, everything starts in the spirit world according to II Corinthians, chapter 4:18, which lets us know, that we cannot put trust in the things that we see, but rather, we should put our trust in the things that we do not see, because the things that we see are temporal, but the things that we do not see are eternal.

Every word that comes out of your mouth, when speaking to a certain thing or condition, or giving a directive, or answering a question, should be spoken with a calculated purpose, to gain an expected result.

This means you should be slow to speak and quick to listen (James 1:19). Some say that you should take the time to taste your words before you let them out.

In Matthew, chapter 8:8-9, "We read the account of great faith and how it works. The centurion answered and said, "Lord, I am not worthy that you should come under my roof: but speak the word only, and my servant shall be healed.

Because I am a man under authority, having soldiers under me: and I say to this man, Go, and he will go, and to another, Come, and he comes; and to my servant, do this, and he does it." In verse 10, Jesus calls this, great faith, and in verse 13, He tells the centurion to go back to his home, and as he has believed, it shall be done, and as he went, his servant was healed in that same hour. Why?

This man heard about Jesus and the great works that was being done by Him, and this man believed that Jesus could do the same for his servant, based on the fact that he and Jesus were on the same level, but working for two different kingdoms. He starts out by saying, that he is a man under authority (the authority given to him by the roman king), and that he recognized that Jesus was under authority (the authority given to Him by God).

Please take note: In order to be in authority, you must first be under authority. The roman centurion was in authority because he was given authority by the roman government, and all of the men that was assigned to him as soldiers, were subject to his word, all he had to do was speak the word and whatever he said, it was done.

Well, this man recognized that Jesus was under the authority given to Him by the Father. Acts, chapter 10:38 says, God anointed Jesus of Nazareth with the Holy Ghost and with power.

In Philippians, chapter 2:9, God has highly exalted him, and gave him a name that is above all other names. In verse 10, that at the name of Jesus every knee should bow, of things in heaven, and in earth, and things under the earth.

Verse 11: "And that every tongue should confess that Jesus Christ is Lord, to the glory of God the Father. In Matthew, chapter 28:18, Jesus says this, "All power is given unto me in heaven and in earth."

The roman centurion also realized that Jesus was operating in the realm of the spirit world, and that the spirit world had more power than the natural and that the spirit world was under Jesus' authority and whatever he said, it was done by those in the spirit world.

Section 15

The Enemy of Faith

I f there is a good, then there is an opposing bad, and if these two exist, then there is a choice.

In a normal setting, the spirit of faith can be stopped by the spirit of unbelief. Look at Matthew, chapter 13:58, it is recorded here that Jesus could not do many mighty works there because of their unbelief.

The spirit of unbelief is able to do that because what Jesus said in Mark, chapter 4, when He explains the parable of the sower sowing the Word. Satan and his kingdom of darkness come to steal the Word. Remember, God has to confirm His word in you and if there is no Word in you, He cannot confirm anything. And since He cannot confirm His word in you, faith cannot give the command to the spirits of God or the angels of God to go forth and do what you are saying.

Your words are not like God's Words, whereby they can create things from the spirit. Only God's words can do that, but what your words can do is command, express, reveal, request, incite, calm, and hinder; affecting both the natural and the spiritual world, both will begin to respond to what you are saying to some degree.

Now, here is where things can get sticky, if you let it. Living things can respond to you because they were created by God, man-made things can respond to you in very small ways because they were made by man. For example: It has been proven that flowers, animals, and trees can respond to a continued voice command. Even amazing, is how your car performs when you speak to it.

Why is this? All things are made up of atoms, and those atoms were made by God, and they have the ability to respond to the vibrations of the sounds of your words, but that is on a small scale. Remember, there is no magic, only knowledge, understanding, and wisdom. Your words do not carry physical force like God's Words, but what they can't do physically, they can command spiritually.

Remember this; we are dealing with two sets of laws: the spiritual laws and the natural laws. And in order to effectively use them, you must know them and respect them, because to break either could put you in deep peril.

Now getting back to the way things get done in the spirit world. The Roman centurion's servant was not there to hear what was said, so his flesh and his spirit had nothing to do with his healing, but he was healed. Why?

The Roman centurion only asked that Jesus would speak the word only and he explained why. Jesus said to the man that he had great faith, then he told the man to go his way and as he has believed, that is how it was going to be, and in that same instant the man's servant was healed. How did the servant get healed, when he was not there to hear the word being given or the laying on by hands taking place?

Faith had the go ahead from God because the word was confirmed in this man's heart. So faith could tell the spirit of health to go and rebuke the spirit of sickness, so that the man's body could return to good health.

In Mark, chapter 11:24, Jesus says this, "Because of this, I say to you, that whatever you desire, when you pray, believe that you will get it, and you shall receive it."

Faith has to have the confirmation of God's Word in your heart, and in order for the Word of God to be in your heart, you must hear the Word and believe it first. Then you can act on faith by speaking what you desire based on what you have received and believed about God and the power of words.

Your words can take on three positions: they can take the position of belief or they can take the position of unbelief or they can take the position of being neutral, which is doing nothing at all. In either case, God will hold you accountable for your words position in life. Matthew, chapter 12:36, Jesus says this, "Every idle (inactive, unassigned, neutral, and unemployed) word that men shall speak, they shall give account thereof in the Day of Judgment."

If you will have to give an account for your words, then doesn't it make good sense to make sure that you use your words with wisdom, knowledge, and understanding?

People say many things in the run of a day, but how much of what you say is something that God can use?

Section 16

Hearing the word

I f you can hear, then you can learn, and if you can learn, then you can achieve.

There seems to be a formula to the use of faith, and that formula is this: You must first hear the Word, which comes by preaching or teaching the Word: Matthew, chapter 9:35 says, "Jesus went about all the cities and villages, teaching in their synagogues, and preaching the gospel of the kingdom, and healing every sickness and every disease among the people." And in chapter 10:7, He tells His disciples to go, and preach the good news of the kingdom, and heal the sick, clean the lepers, raise the dead, and cast out devils.

Romans, chapter 10:17 says this: Faith comes by you hearing the Word of God on continuous bases. You must hear the Word repeatedly so that your mind is renewed and changed from your former way of thinking to God's way of thinking. Romans, chapter 12:2 says this, "Be not conformed to this world: but be ye transformed by the renewing of your mind, that you may prove what is that good, and acceptable, and perfect, will of God."

God's perfect will for you is to learn His Word and when you do, your mind becomes renewed and your former way of thinking is washed away and all things become new. II Corinthians, chapter 5:17, puts it this way: You become a new creature (something that has not existed before), you become a regenerated soul capable of living a type of God kind of life in the earth, and the world will not know who you are in spirit, because they did not know who Jesus was in spirit either.

All things become new to you -- your way of living, your way of thinking, your way of doing things, your way speaking, your way of acting, all these things change with your change. While people may know who you are as a person, they will not recognize who you have become spiritually. You now command a spiritual respect in the spirit world and it is witnessed by the people in the natural world.

Conclusion

C onclusions are always temporal, but opportunities are always growing.

It is my prayer that after reading this book you will come away with a better grip on life and a greater understanding of God and how He deals with and through mankind.

Many people think that God is not fair or that He only cares about who He can find doing the wrong thing, so He can "hit them up" with His anger and revenge; because it is God who they blame for the bad things that happens to them or the natural disasters that has taken so many lives.

Now, if you look back on your life, you will see that many of those bad things came from what you said or the things you did or did not do in certain situations, and from the choices that you made.

My hope is that you will take this book and use it as a guide to change the way you live your life by redirecting the way you speak to yourself and to others, now that you know the value in what you say and how it can affect your life and the lives of others.

Remember this; the past is just that, it is the past, you cannot change it, it is a segment of time that you have stepped through, a string of events that has happened to you that records your past in the pictures of your mind, filed away for you to draw upon for future reference.

What stands before you now is your future and the only way that you can make it good is by what you say and do today. You hold the keys and they are in your mind and in your heart.

What choice of words are you going to let flow from your mouth today?

Take a moment to picture this thought; what you were yesterday does not have to dictate what you will be tomorrow, and what you become on tomorrow, does not have to dictate what you will become in the future.

To Oder More Copies, Please Email Us At:

Willieman2u@hotmail.com